550
BRA

EARTH SCIENCE LIBRARY
PLANET EARTH
MARTYN BRAMWELL

Franklin Watts
London · New York · Toronto · Sydney

© 1987 Franklin Watts

First published in Great Britain by
Franklin Watts
12a Golden Square
London W1

First published in the USA by
Franklin Watts Inc.
387 Park Avenue South
New York, N.Y. 10016

First published in Australia by
Franklin Watts Australia
14 Mars Road
Lane Cove
NSW 2066

UK ISBN: 0 86313 523 4
US ISBN: 0-531-10346-3
Library of Congress Catalog Card
No: 86-51228

Printed in Belgium

Designed by Ben White

Picture Research by
Mick Alexander

Illustrations:
Chris Forsey
Colin Newman/Linden Artists

Photographs:
Ardea 8r, 17, 21
British Museum of Natural History
  (Geological Museum) 27br
Bruce Coleman 7r, 20, 27tl
Robert Estall 10,13
Geo Science Features 11l, 22, 23t,
  24, 25
Robert Harding 26
Frank Lane 14, 15
NASA 1, 5, 7b, 11r
Natural Science Photos back
  cover, 16
ZEFA 8l, 23b, 28, 29

EARTH SCIENCE LIBRARY
PLANET EARTH

Contents

The Sun's family	4
Earth and Moon	6
The changing seasons	8
The restless oceans	10
Earth's atmosphere	12
Highs and lows	14
Shaping the landscape	16
Plant and animal life	18
Clues to the past	20
Minerals and crystals	22
Rocks from the Earth's interior	24
Secondhand rocks	26
Riches from the Earth	28
Glossary	30
Index	32

The Sun's family

▽ Our Galaxy is 100,000 **light years** across. The Sun lies about 30,000 light years from the center, far out on one of the spiral arms.

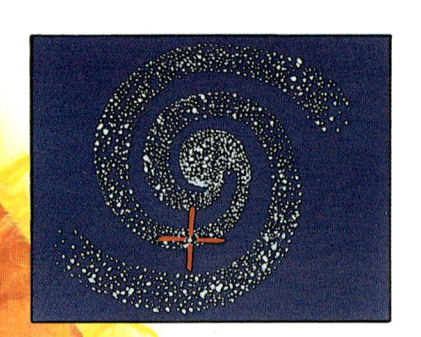

Planet Earth is one of a group of nine planets that circle, or orbit, the Sun. Together they make up the Sun's family – the **Solar System**.

Our Sun is really just an ordinary medium-sized star – one of the 100 billion that make up the Milky Way **Galaxy**. To us it appears to be the biggest object in the heavens, but that is simply because it is so much closer than any other star. It lies just 150 million km (93 million miles) away, and its light reaches us in just over eight minutes. Light from the next nearest star takes well over four *years* to reach the Earth.

1 Mercury: 4,900 km (3,045 miles) in diameter. No atmosphere. Hot enough to melt tin. Heavily cratered.

3 Earth: 12,756 km (7,925 miles) in diameter. Atmosphere, rich in oxygen and water vapor. Abundant life.

2 Venus: 12,100 km (7,520 miles) across. Very hot, poisonous atmosphere with swirling clouds of acid.

4 Mars: 6,790 km (4,220 miles) in diameter. Covered in red stony deserts. Bitterly cold. No water except for ice caps.

The planets vary enormously in size and composition. The four innermost ones are small and rocky, but only Earth supports life. Mercury and Venus are too near the Sun and therefore too hot, while Mars is too far away and therefore too cold.

Beyond Mars lies the asteroid belt – a band of orbiting rock fragments ranging from stones to mini-planets 1,000 km (620 miles) across.

Next come the much bigger outer planets, Jupiter, Saturn, Uranus and Neptune. These are made mainly of dense gases and are often called the gas giants. Farthest out of all lies Pluto. It is smaller than our Moon and probably made of ice.

△ This stunning photograph from the Apollo 17 Moonflight mission shows the crescent Earth rising over the Moon's horizon, lit from one side by the Sun. It shows how well the Earth deserves its name, the Blue Planet.

5 Jupiter: 142,800 km (88,750 miles) in diameter. A huge ball of liquid hydrogen hidden under hick swirling gas clouds.

7 Uranus: 50,800 km (31,500 miles) across. The **axis** of spin is tilted right over so Uranus seems to lie on its side.

6 Saturn: 120,000 km (75,000 miles) in diameter. Largely gas with a rocky core. The rings are of ice and rock fragments.

8 Neptune: 48,600 km (30,200 miles) in diameter. Smallest of the gas giants. Neptune orbits the Sun every 165 years.

9 Pluto: 2,400 km (1,500 miles) in diameter. Thought to be made of ice. It was only discovered in 1930.

Earth and Moon

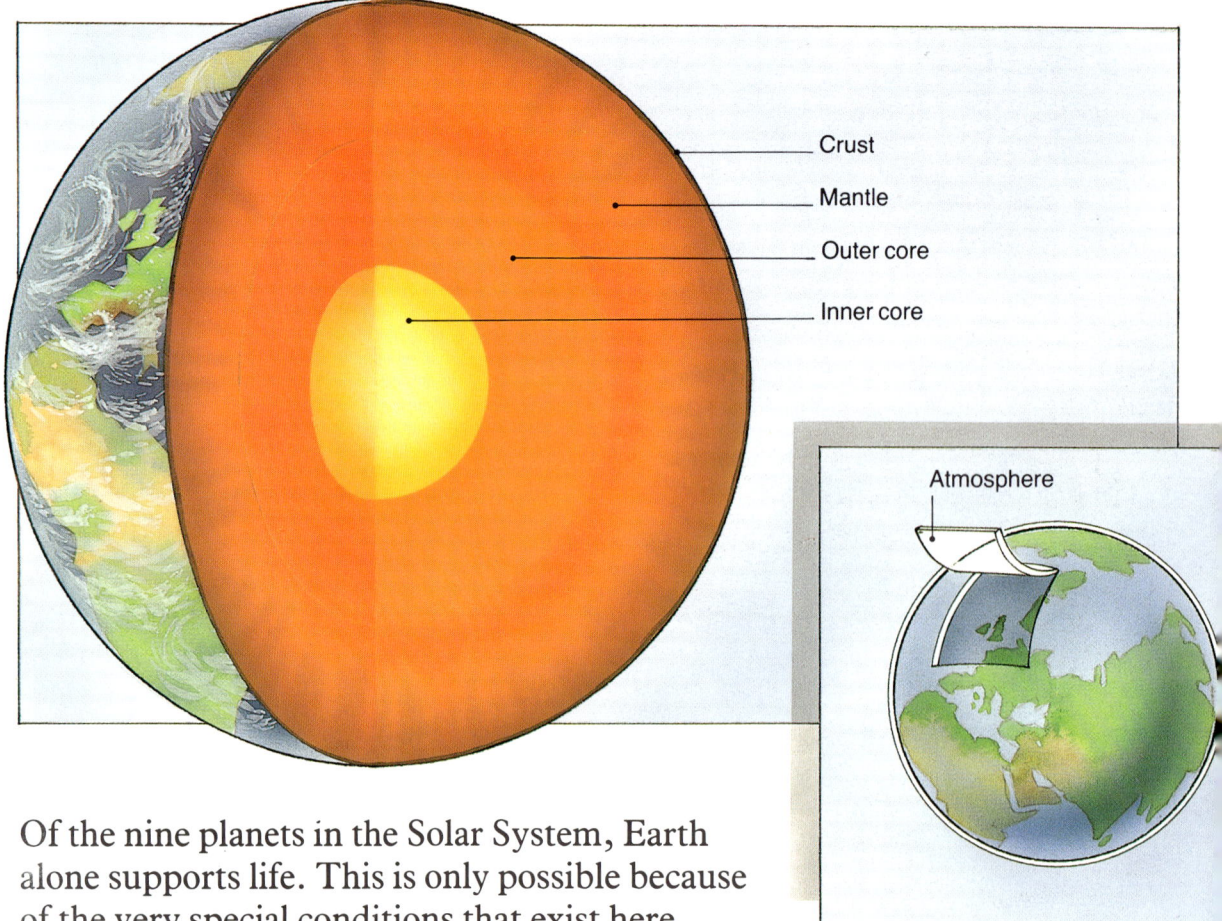

Crust
Mantle
Outer core
Inner core

Atmosphere

Of the nine planets in the Solar System, Earth alone supports life. This is only possible because of the very special conditions that exist here.

Earth's orbit around the Sun is almost perfectly circular. This means that we are always roughly the same distance from the Sun, so our planet does not suffer from wild extremes of heat and cold. Our orbit is also just the right distance from the Sun to allow liquid water to exist on the surface. Much closer and the water would be evaporated away by the heat: much farther away and it would all be locked up as ice.

This combination of moderate temperatures, water, and the huge variety of chemical building blocks held in the Earth's rocks provided the starting point for life to evolve on Earth.

△ The outermost layer of the Earth is the thin hard **crust** on which we live. Below that is the **mantle** – part solid, part molten, and very hot. At the center lie the liquid outer **core** and solid inner core – both made mainly of iron.

Without the atmosphere *(inset)* no life could exist on Earth, yet it is surprisingly thin – barely the thickness of a layer of paint on a model globe.

Many of the planets have natural satellites, or moons. Mars, for example, has two, while Jupiter has at least 14. Our own planet has one constant companion – the Moon. It has no atmosphere. There is no air, no water, and therefore no life. The craters that cover the **lunar** landscape were formed millions of years ago by showers of **meteorites** crashing into the surface. Many were stones and small boulders, but some were many kilometers in diameter – exploding on impact with the force of atomic bombs and leaving craters more than 200 km (125 miles) across. The dark, smooth areas on the Moon are ancient **lava** flows.

The Moon turns on its axis once every $27\frac{1}{3}$ days – exactly the same time it takes to make one journey around the Earth. The result is that the same side always faces toward the Earth. Not until the dawn of the Space Age was man able to take a look at the far side of the Moon.

△ A partial **eclipse** occurs when the Moon passes between the Sun and Earth, covering part of the Sun's disc and casting a shadow on the Earth. In a total eclipse, the bright disc of the Sun is blotted out completely.

◁ In July 1969 astronauts Neil Armstrong and Edwin (Buzz) Aldrin made history when they set foot on the Moon's surface. Here, Aldrin carefully makes his way down the ladder from the Lunar Landing Module.

The changing seasons

In the cool temperate lands lying between the hot tropics and the cold polar regions, plant and animal life changes throughout the year. In spring the trees are bright green with new growth. In summer they are heavy with leaves, flowers and fruits. In autumn growth stops, and the leaves turn brown, finally falling to the ground and leaving the trees bare as winter sets in.

But the seasons are not the same all over the globe. Tropical lands are warm throughout the year, with very little change. In the polar regions six months of winter darkness and cold alternate with six months of continuous day. Plant growth and animal activity are compressed into a few months in midsummer.

▽ Tropical rainforest, like this area of the Amazon jungle in South America, is dense and green throughout the year. Animal, bird and insect life is rich and varied because a plentiful supply of food is always available.

◁ The midnight Sun shines down on a frozen expanse of sea off the Greenland coast. In the far north, the seasons are harsh. The few land animals that live there are specially adapted to survive the winter cold.

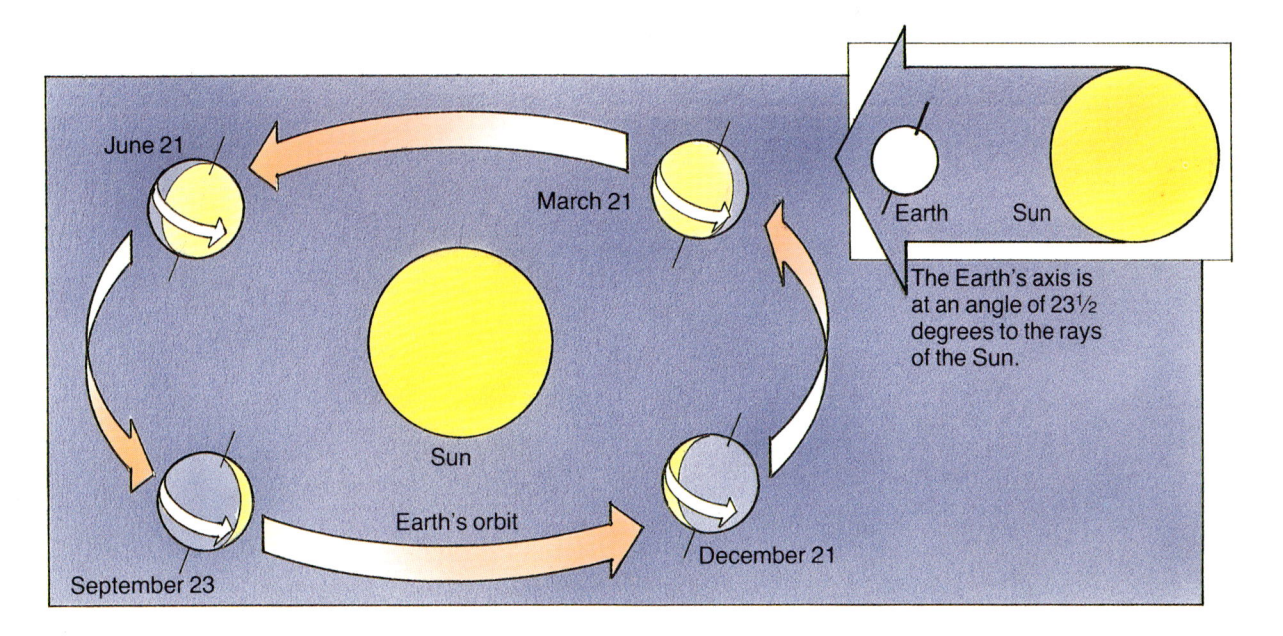

Figure labels: June 21, March 21, Sun, Earth's orbit, September 23, December 21, Earth, Sun. The Earth's axis is at an angle of 23½ degrees to the rays of the Sun.

To discover the cause of the seasons we must look again at the Earth in its orbit around the Sun. The Earth travels once around the Sun each year. It is also spinning on its own axis, once every 24 hours. As it spins, one side of the globe is lit by the Sun and is in daylight; the other side is turned away from the Sun and is in darkness.

If the Earth's axis were upright, compared with its path around the Sun, day and night would be the same length all over the world, and there would be no seasons. But the Earth's axis is not upright. It is tilted at 23½ degrees so that the globe is unevenly lit. In summer, when the Earth is at one end of its annual journey, the northern **hemisphere** is tilted toward the Sun. The days are long and the nights are short. North of the Arctic Circle the Sun never sets.

In winter, at the opposite end of the journey, the northern regions are tilted away from the Sun. Nights are long, and the days short and cool.

The tropical regions, close to the **Equator**, are evenly lit at all times of the year and so have hardly any seasonal changes.

△ The small diagram above shows how the tilt of the Earth's axis causes the globe to be lit unevenly by the rays of the Sun.

The larger diagram shows the Earth's annual journey around the Sun. In June it is summer in the northern hemisphere and winter in the southern hemisphere. September is autumn in the north, but spring for those living south of the Equator. By December it is the turn of the southern hemisphere to face the Sun, while the northern regions shiver through their winter. And in March the cycle is completed, with spring in the north and autumn in the south.

The restless oceans

Earthquakes and volcanic eruptions are probably the most spectacular short-term events in the natural world, but for sheer continuous power look no farther than the edge of the seas. The oceans are never still. Even on a mirror-calm day the water is in motion. The surface may appear quite still, but just a few meters below the surface, currents may be sweeping along the coast faster than a man can run.

When strong winds drive waves against the shore, the full power of the sea is revealed. Wave after wave rears up and then crashes against the coastline, splitting rocks apart, piling up sand and pebbles in one place as fast as it is sweeping them away somewhere else.

Nothing remains unchanged for long in nature, and wherever sea meets land the water is at work, constantly shaping and reshaping the shoreline.

△ Even in good weather some parts of the coast may still be battered by large waves. This stretch of the coast of Portugal has no protection. It faces out into the Atlantic, and these incoming waves may have been born hundreds of kilometers out to sea in some distant storm.

▷ A satellite view of a hurricane off the North American coast. Heat and moisture picked up over the warm Caribbean Sea provided the energy for this revolving storm.

▽ This large sand and gravel spit has been built up over many years by currents sweeping along the coast at Cape Hatteras in North Carolina. The older parts of the spit have already been colonized by shoreline vegetation.

Waves wear away the coastal rocks in several ways. Millions of tons of water crashing repeatedly against a cliff weaken the rocks. Air trapped beneath the breakers is rammed into cracks in the rocks with explosive force. Rock fragments already loosened are picked up by following waves and hurled back again, breaking off more pieces and being broken up themselves.

Even the gentler waves of fair weather are at work, constantly rolling pebbles back and forth. Corners are knocked off. The pebbles become smooth and rounded, but all the time they are being worn away. Eventually, lumps of even the hardest rocks may be worn down to fine sand.

But the seas can build as well as destroy. Sand and pebbles from one stretch of coast may be swept along by waves and currents. And when the force of the current slackens, the load is dropped, to build into pebble banks, sand bars and spits.

The seas are also the power-house of weather systems. They soak up the heat of the Sun, then release it back into the atmosphere to fuel the swirling clouds that sweep across the oceans.

Earth's atmosphere

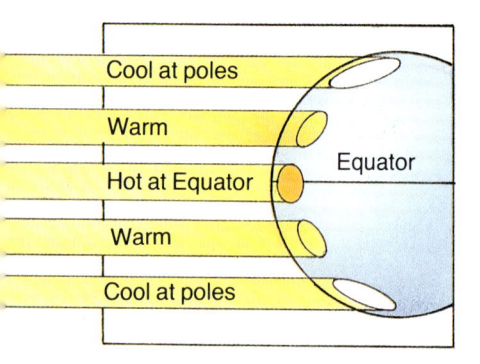

If you throw a ball into the air, it quickly falls back to Earth. It is pulled back by the force of **gravity**. That same invisible force holds our atmosphere in place. Without it, the life-giving oxygen and water vapor, the nitrogen and other gases would all drift off into space.

We cannot see the Earth's atmosphere, and we can feel it only when the wind blows. Yet it is all around us. We live at the bottom of an "ocean" of air that extends more than 1,000 km (620 miles) outward from the Earth's surface.

Just like the watery oceans, the atmosphere is constantly in motion. Some parts are warmer than others, and the warm air rises. Some parts are cooler, and the cold air sinks. Surface winds and high-altitude wind systems encircle the globe in well-defined patterns, very like the current systems of the world's great oceans.

The deeper you go in any ocean, the greater the pressure becomes. That is because the pressure is caused by the weight of water above you.

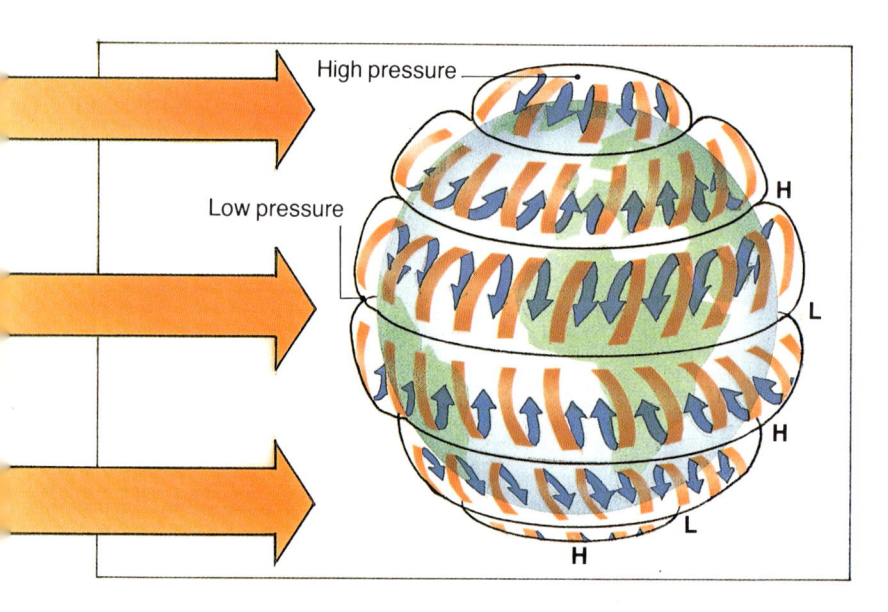

△ Imagine the Sun's rays to be like a series of beams from a flashlight. Beams hitting the Earth near the Equator make concentrated circular patches of light, but those hitting the more steeply curved polar regions spread out into larger oval patches. This is why tropical regions are always warmer than polar regions.

◁ Hot air rising near the Equator spreads out to north and south at high levels, then sinks back toward the surface. Rising air reduces the pressure at the surface, creating low-pressure areas. Sinking air presses down harder and creates "highs." And because winds always blow from high-pressure areas to low, the surface winds blow back toward the Equator. Similar wind "cells" encircle the globe in the temperate and polar regions.

The same is true in our "ocean" of air. Pressure is greatest at the bottom – at the Earth's surface – and gets less the higher you go. Because we are adapted to it we cannot feel this air pressure, yet at sea level more than a kilogram of air is pressing on every square centimeter of our bodies.

There are traces of atmospheric gases as far out as 1,000 km (620 miles), but most of the atmosphere is squashed into a thin surface layer. Roughly three-quarters of the atmosphere lies below the level of Mount Everest's summit, and even at about 5,500 m (18,000 ft) the air is so thin that few people can breathe easily without additional supplies of oxygen.

Without the atmosphere there would be no life – and that is not just because of the lack of oxygen. The atmosphere also protects us. It shields us from dangerous radiation from the Sun, and it provides a "blanket" that holds in some of the Sun's heat through the hours of darkness.

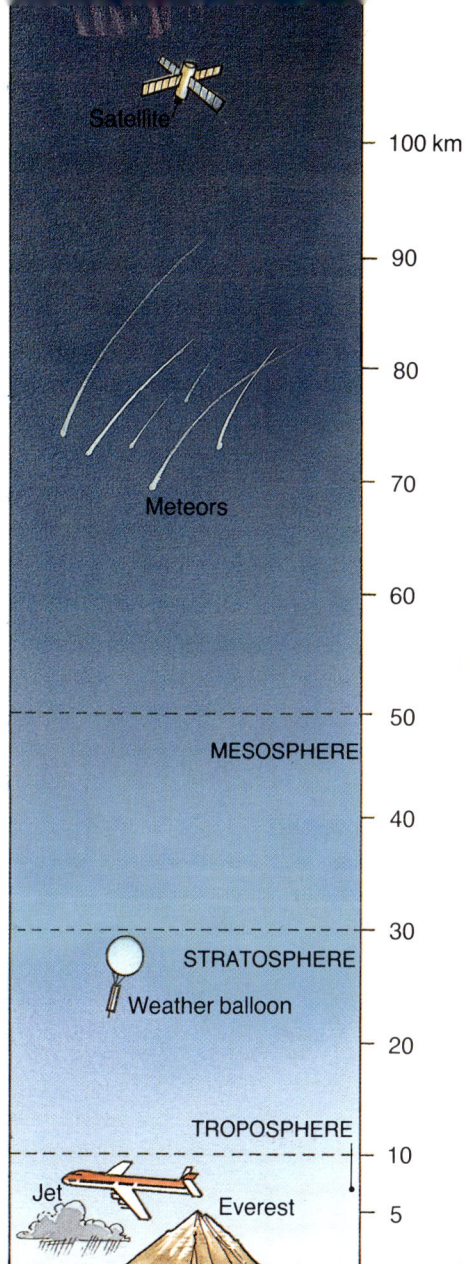

△ The atmosphere is divided into a number of layers. The coldest part is at 80 km (50 miles) **altitude**, where the temperature is −100°C. Everything we call "weather" occurs in the first few kilometers of atmosphere.

◁ Despite strict laws in many countries, air pollution is a big environmental problem.

Highs and lows

The high- and low-pressure areas on a weather forecaster's chart indicate very different kinds of weather, and one of the best clues to look for is the amount and type of cloud.

Air always contains a certain amount of water vapor. The warmer the air is, the more water vapor it can hold. But only up to a point. Once the air is **saturated**, any extra water vapor **condenses** out into billions of microscopic water droplets. It is these droplets, drifting in the air, that we see as clouds.

High-pressure areas occur where cool air sinks toward the Earth's surface. As it sinks, the air becomes warmer. It can hold more moisture as it warms up and so there are very few clouds.

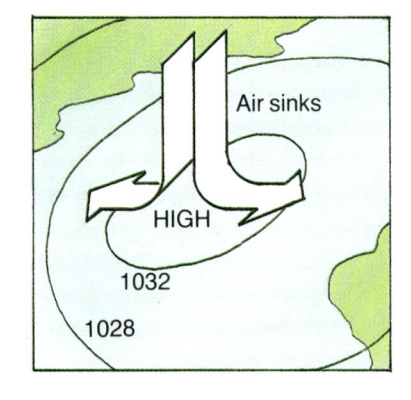

▽ Scattered fluffy *cumulus* clouds are typical of the settled fair weather that often accompanies summer highs. Winter highs bring cold clear weather conditions.

The typical weather of a summer high is a clear blue sky dotted with small fluffy white clouds. Temperatures are often very high, and winds are light. Winds blow outward from high-pressure areas, but the Earth's spin pushes the wind off course. The result is that northern hemisphere winds blow clockwise around a high. Southern hemisphere winds blow counterclockwise.

In low-pressure systems the air is rising and cooling. Thick layers of cloud develop, and the excess water usually falls as rain, hail or snow. Lows often start where a large mass of warm air meets a large mass of cold air. A kink forms in the boundary, and this eventually grows into the familiar warm and cold **fronts** of a **depression**.

The winds in a low-pressure system try to blow inward, but because of Earth's spin they blow counterclockwise in the northern hemisphere and clockwise in the southern hemisphere.

△ Heavy black *cumulonimbus* stormclouds darken the sky as a thunderstorm sweeps across the grasslands of East Africa. Brief but violent storms are often caused by hot air rising over the sun-baked plains.

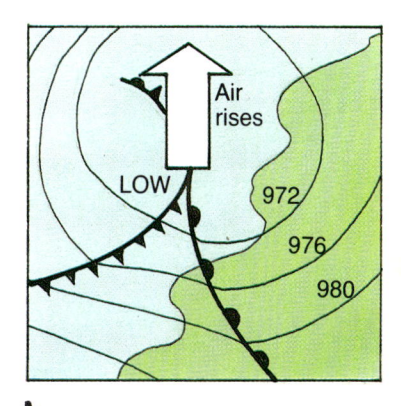

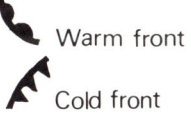

Warm front
Cold front

Shaping the landscape

While the seas are battering away at the edges of the land, other forces are at work far inland, shaping the hills and valleys and plains.

Three main processes are involved. *Erosion* is the process of breaking down the rocks into small fragments. *Transportation* is the process of carrying this debris away. And *deposition* is the process of laying down layers of gravel, sand and mud in lowland areas and around the coast.

These processes are very slow, but nature is in no hurry. It has all the millions of years it needs. In temperate regions the main force of erosion is running water. Even small mountain streams wear away at the rocks, but farther down, when the stream has grown into a river, its power is hundreds of times greater. Mud, sand and pebbles swept along by the water scrape away at the bed and sides of the river, constantly widening and deepening its valley.

In high mountains and polar regions freezing cold and moving ice are the great sculptors. Water melted by the Sun trickles into cracks in the rocks. When the temperature falls at night, the water freezes. Because water expands when it turns to ice, the cracks are forced open and pieces of rock are split off. These shattered fragments tumble on to the glaciers below and are carried away. Frozen into the moving ice, they help the **glacier** gouge its deep U-shaped valley.

Desert rocks are split by the rapid heating and cooling caused by blistering daytime heat and night temperatures that plunge below zero. Loose sand is blasted against other rocks by constant gales, and deep valleys are carved by the **flash floods** that follow desert rainstorms.

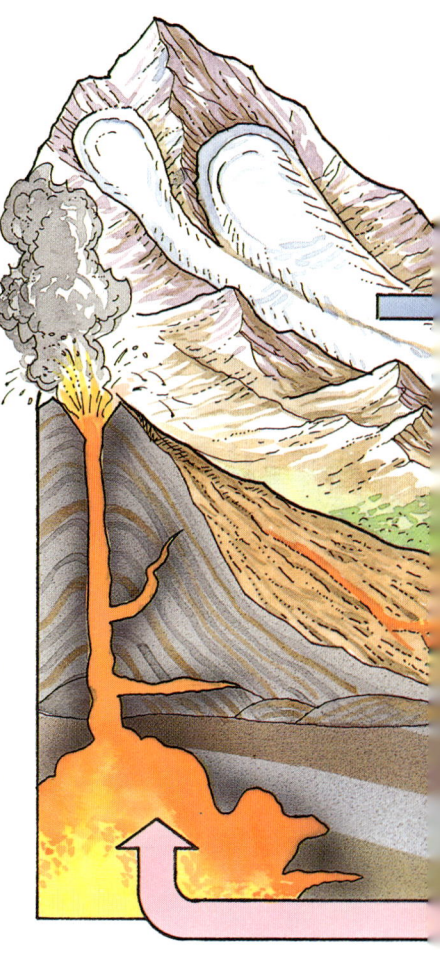

△ The processes that shape the Earth's surface are part of a never-ending cycle. Eroded fragments of rock are carried into the sea and are slowly buried. After millions of years, chemical changes turn them back into solid rock. One day they will be forced back to the surface – and the process of erosion will start all over again.

▷ Eroded cliffs and pinnacles of pink and white limestone, shale and sandstone in Utah's Bryce Canyon National Park.

▷ In its final approach to the sea a river usually flows over fairly level ground. It loses speed – and also its ability to carry its load of sand and silt. Where the river flows into the sea, it may build a broad fan-shaped area of sand called a delta, like this one at the mouth of the King River in western Tasmania.

Plant and animal life

▷ The map shows the present-day pattern of vegetation zones around the world.

But the world has not always looked like this. Coal seams in Antarctica prove that the icy southern continent was once partly covered by swamp forests. Other geological clues prove that southern India once lay beneath an ice-sheet.

This does not mean that Earth's vegetation zones have changed position. It is the continents that have moved over the Earth's surface – like pieces of a moving jigsaw puzzle.

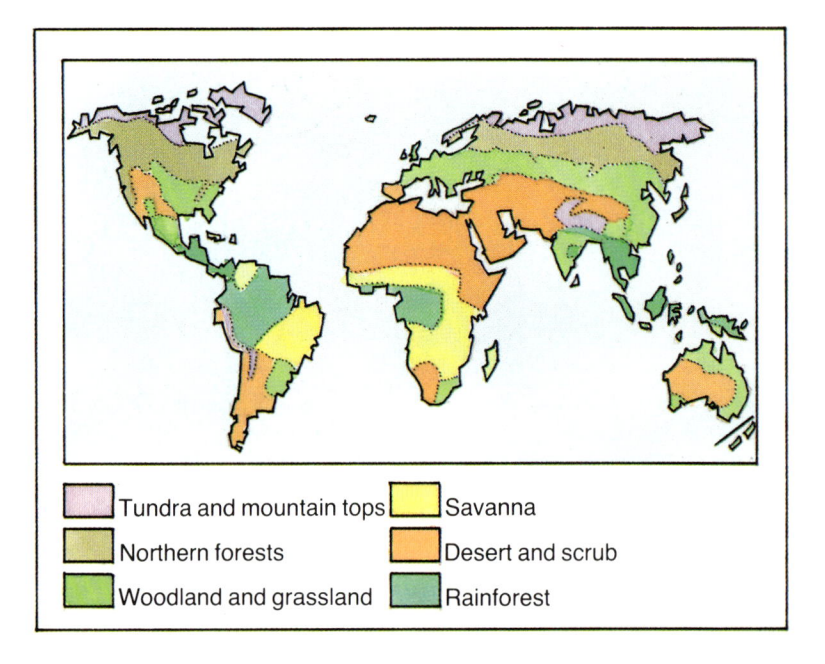

Tundra and mountain tops
Northern forests
Woodland and grassland
Savanna
Desert and scrub
Rainforest

The broad bands of vegetation that encircle the Earth are controlled mainly by climate. In simple terms the hot, wet tropical areas support dense rainforests. The mild temperate regions support grasslands and seasonal woodlands. And the cold regions of the far north support little but the mosses and lichens of the Arctic **tundra**. In between there are hot deserts and cold deserts, marshlands and **savannas**. Each one is a living system – an **ecosystem** – created by its special combination of climate, soil, plants and animals.

The animals of each zone are adapted to take advantage of conditions there. Forest hunters are agile climbers or builders of traps and snares. Those of the grasslands are sharp-eyed and sharp-eared, relying on speed or ambush. The plant-eaters are even more specialized, ranging from earthworms and hummingbirds, monkeys and mice, to elephants, termites and snails.

Woodland and grassland
The woods and grasslands of the temperate zone support squirrels, foxes, moles, voles and shrews, and a host of bird and insect life.

Our planet supports an amazing variety of plant and animal life. So far, scientists have named well over a quarter of a million different plant **species**, and there must be tens or even hundreds of thousands more still waiting to be discovered.

About one million animals are known to science. Well over three-quarters of these are insects, and most of the rest are worms, jellyfish, snails, crabs and centipedes. These are the invertebrates – the animals without backbones.

The vertebrates, or backboned animals, may be outnumbered by the rest, but they include all the "higher" animals – those with complex bodies and more advanced brains. They include about 20,000 fish species, 8,600 birds, 6,000 reptiles and 4,200 mammals – our own animal group.

African savanna
Vast expanses of grassland dotted with clumps of flat-topped acacia trees are the habitat of lions, cheetahs, zebras and antelopes.

Tundra and northern forest
The harsh northern lands are home to Arctic hares and foxes, snowy owls and lemmings, as well as huge herds of caribou, musk ox and reindeer.

Tropical rainforest
The dense green jungles support the richest life of all. Thousands of plant and animal species have still to be studied. Many could benefit mankind.

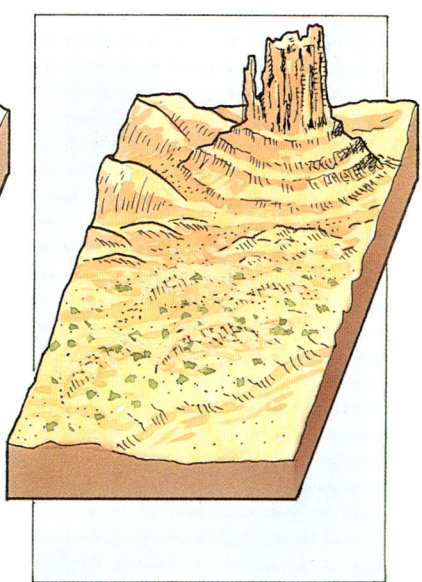

Desert and scrubland
The world's dry lands have a surprisingly rich animal life – from burrowing mice, lizards and snakes to antelopes and eagles.

Clues to the past

Hidden in the rocks beneath our feet is an almost unbroken record of life on Earth stretching back more than 600 million years into the past.

That record is provided by fossils – the remains of plants and animals preserved in layers of mud, sand and limestone laid down millions of years ago in ancient rivers, lakes and seas.

When an animal died in the water, its body would sink to the bottom. The soft fleshy parts would quickly rot away or be eaten by other animals, but shells and bones were often covered by sediments. Slowly, over millions of years, chemical changes have altered these remains, turning them into fossils – often as hard as stone, but preserving every detail of the original animal.

Fortunately for us these **sedimentary rocks** are frequently forced back to the Earth's surface. And as erosion wears them away, the fossils are revealed to tell their fascinating story.

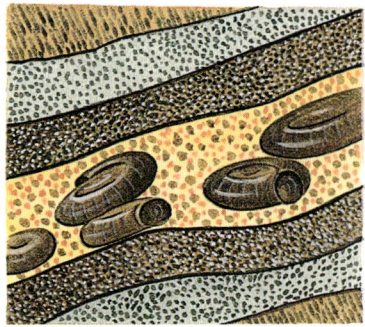

△ In this reconstruction an **ammonite** dies and sinks to the sea bed. Along with many others it is buried, and very slowly the mud hardens around the shells, forming a perfect fossil like those shown on the left.

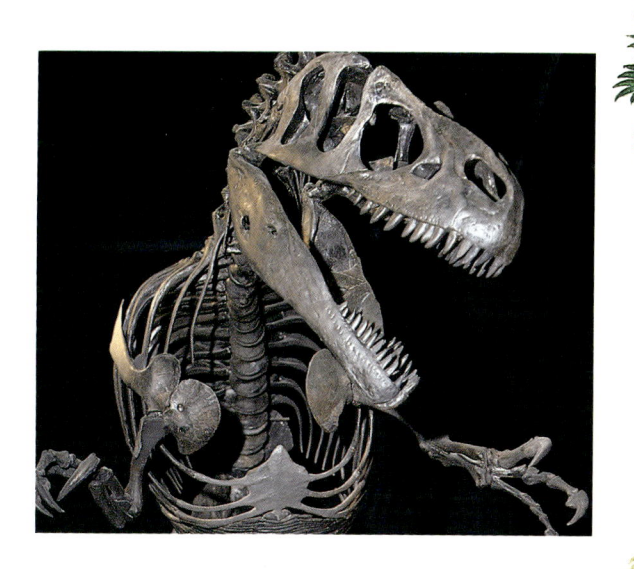

At 12 m (40 ft) long and up to 5 m (16 ft) high, the two-ton flesh-eating *Allosaurus* was one of the most fearsome dinosaurs of all. It lived about 150 million years ago.

Scientists have built up a picture of these huge animals by carefully piecing together fossilized bones and teeth.

As well as teeth and bones, stems and leaves, many other objects and events can be recorded in the Earth's rocks. Dinosaur eggs have been found. So have dinosaur droppings. Animal footprints have been preserved, and so have the trails left in sea-bed mud by crawling animals.

Fossil ripple-marks reveal ancient shorelines. Marks in the sand of dried-up river beds show which way the rivers flowed. Even traces of magnetism in rocks can reveal how the continents themselves have moved over the Earth's surface.

Fossils are enormously useful. They not only provide clues about what Earth looked like in the past, they also help us to date rocks and to compare rock layers in places a long way apart.

Minerals and crystals

◁ Pyrite, or iron pyrites, is a combination of iron and sulfur. It is a very common mineral of iron, but is not used to make iron and steel because the sulfur makes it difficult to process.

Minerals are the main chemical building blocks from which all the different kinds of rock are made. They in turn are combinations of smaller chemical building blocks called **elements**.

Some minerals consist entirely of one element. These are called native elements and include gold, which occurs as a pure native element, diamond, which is pure carbon, and sulfur – the strong-smelling yellow substance often found encrusted around small holes in the sides of certain types of volcano.

Most minerals, however, are mixtures of elements. Quartz, the most important rock-forming mineral of all, consists of one unit of silicon joined to two of oxygen. Common salt, which is found in some sedimentary rock layers and in seawater, always consists of one unit of sodium combined with one of chloride.

△ Hematite is another iron mineral, this time combined with oxygen. It is one of the chief iron **ores** and therefore one of the world's most important minerals. Unlike pyrites, which forms shiny yellow cube-shaped crystals, this iron mineral forms lumpy masses from which it gets the name "kidney ore." The lumps are made of thousands of small crystals.

Minerals usually occur as small crystals all mixed up together to make a particular kind of rock. **Granite**, for example, is made up mainly of crystals of quartz and two other minerals called feldspar and mica.

Occasionally, however, you may come across large and beautifully shaped crystals. Some are smooth and waxy-looking; others have a metallic shine. Some, like asbestos and gypsum, have a woolly or hairy appearance like frayed cloth, while others form slender pencil-like crystals with glassy sides and pyramid-pointed ends.

Large crystals usually formed where a pocket of molten volcanic rock cooled exceptionally slowly. Among the most attractive are the clusters of crystals that line the insides of geodes – fist- or football-sized hollow cavities sometimes found in masses of dark volcanic **basalt** rock.

△ Native gold, seen here on a large quartz crystal, is usually 85–95% pure.

▽ The main mineral in this beautiful natural crystal rosette is amethyst – a pale violet-colored form of transparent quartz.

Rocks from the Earth's interior

Rocks that first formed in the molten state, deep inside the Earth's crust, are called **igneous rocks** – which means "born of fire."

Most spectacular are the lava flows and **ash** clouds thrown out by volcanoes. These cool and harden into a family of rock types called **extrusive** rocks. On land, ancient lava flows form enormous plateaus like the Deccan in India and the Columbia plateau in the United States.

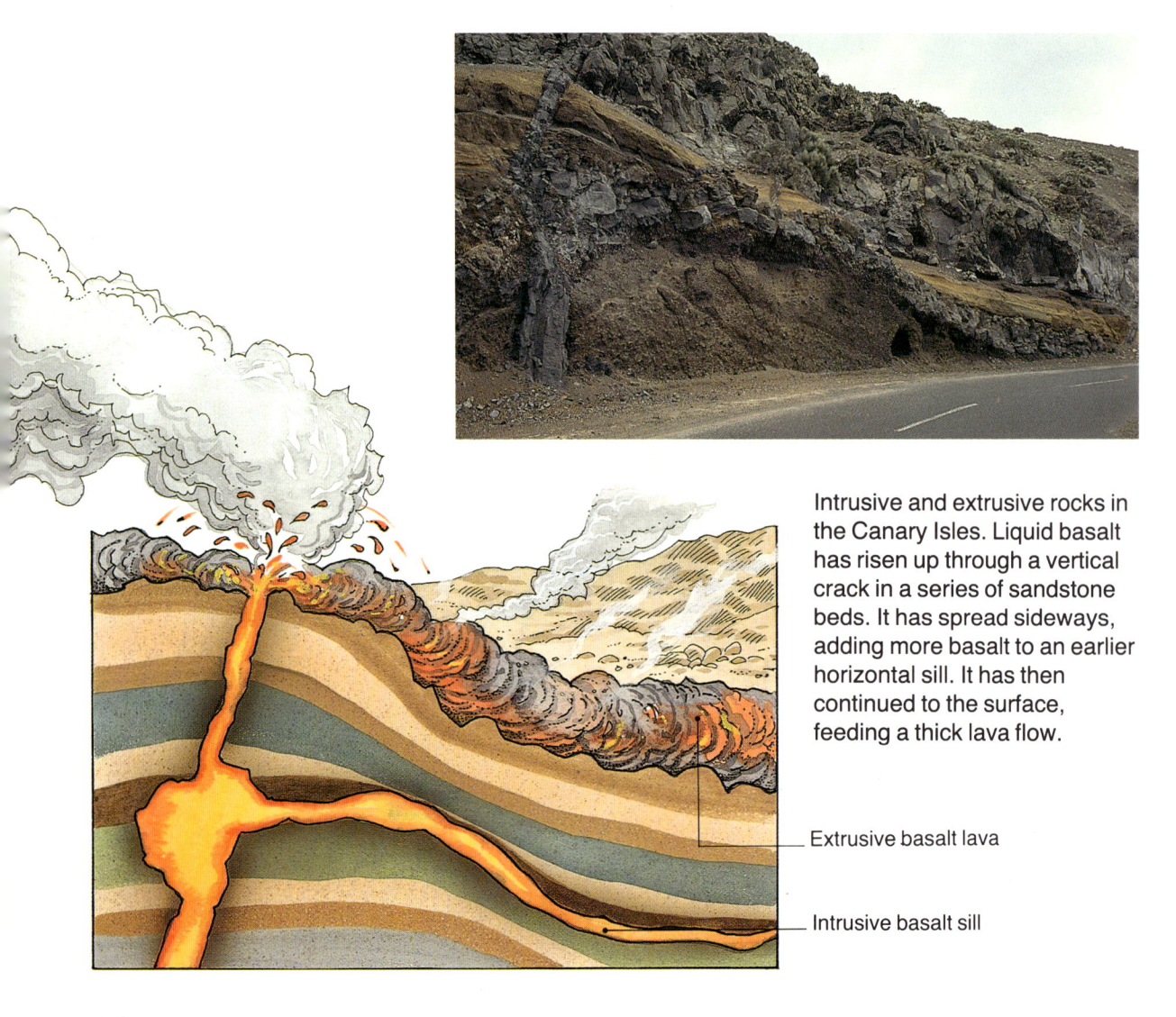

Intrusive and extrusive rocks in the Canary Isles. Liquid basalt has risen up through a vertical crack in a series of sandstone beds. It has spread sideways, adding more basalt to an earlier horizontal sill. It has then continued to the surface, feeding a thick lava flow.

Extrusive basalt lava

Intrusive basalt sill

Another important group, the **intrusive** rocks, are not as obvious – but play just as big a part in shaping the scenery around us.

Intrusive rocks started out molten and began the journey upward toward the Earth's surface. They never made it. Some were squeezed between other rock layers and hardened there as *sills*. Some were forced into cracks cutting through other rock layers: these are called *dykes*. But biggest of all are the **batholiths** of igneous rock – especially granite – that hardened in the upper layers of the crust. Erosion has now exposed the tops of some of these huge intrusions. They form landscape features like Dartmoor in southwest Britain and the huge granite domes of California's Yosemite National Park.

△ Vixen Tor on Dartmoor in southwest Britain. Tors are very characteristic of these granite moorlands. They are isolated masses of rock, usually heavily eroded by wind and rain. The granite develops horizontal and vertical cracks called joints as it cools from the molten state. Later on, when erosion has stripped away the overlying rocks and exposed the granite, these joints are opening up by the **weathering** processes.

25

Secondhand rocks

The second great family of rocks, after the igneous group, is the sedimentary rock family. These can be thought of as secondhand rocks, as in general they are made from earlier, older rocks.

Most sedimentary rocks consist of mud, sand, silt and gravel eroded from ancient landscapes. They are then laid down, or deposited, in layers on the beds of rivers, lakes and seas.

As the sediment is swept into the lake, the heaviest particles settle first, followed by finer and finer layers. By looking closely at a bed of rock, a geologist can tell from the grain size if the bed is the right way up – or if later movements of the Earth's crust have turned the whole bed upside down.

△ You can see the process of sedimentation in a simple experiment. Place some garden soil in a large jar and cover it with water. Stir well, and then let it stand.

After a few hours the heavier grit will have settled. After several days the water will be clear and you will have several more layers, with fine mud at the top.

▷ Two geology lessons in one. These alternating beds of sandstone and mudstone form part of a cliff on the Pembrokeshire coast in Wales. See how the harder sandstone has resisted erosion far better than the soft mudstone and shale. You can also see how Earth movements have turned the whole mass of rock through 90 degrees. (The beds were originally laid down horizontally.)

◁ Blue-gray walls of fine-grained slate surround a deep pool in this abandoned Welsh slate quarry. The slate splits, or cleaves, easily into thin sheets, making it an ideal material for roofing buildings.

▽ Many kinds of limestone and marble are used in buildings for their decorative effect. In this highly polished slab you can see dozens of fossilized ammonite shells. The shells are cemented together by masses of tiny **calcite** crystals.

The layers, or beds, of sedimentary rocks are one of their most obvious features. Geologists call them strata. But the rocks are no longer composed simply of the original grains. As the soft sediment turns to rock, new minerals grow in the tiny spaces between the grains, cementing them firmly together.

Some sedimentary rocks are formed in a different way. Chalk, for example, is a soft white rock composed almost entirely of the shells of tiny sea creatures. Not surprisingly, chalk is a very good rock in which to look for other fossils, such as sea urchins, shells and corals.

Finally, there is a third rock family. These are called **metamorphic rocks** (meta = change, morph = shape). They are old sedimentary rocks that have been altered by heat and pressure. Slate, for example, is metamorphosed mudstone, and marble is limestone altered by intense heat.

Riches from the Earth

Although we take it for granted, soil is probably the most precious resource the Earth has to offer. Throughout the world, millions of square kilometers of land are used for growing food crops. And many millions more are used for grazing animals for their milk and meat.

The temperate regions of the world are lucky. The mild climate and rich natural vegetation have created deep fertile soils that are able to produce large quantities of food. The arid tropical regions are less fortunate. Their soils are often thin, with very little natural vegetation to bind them together and provide natural fertilizer. In long periods of drought, the soil turns to dust. With no grass or trees to protect it, the soil is blown away by the wind, leaving desert.

Soil is a mixture of small rock particles and **humus** – the decomposed remains of plants that have died. The humus binds the soil and helps it to hold water.

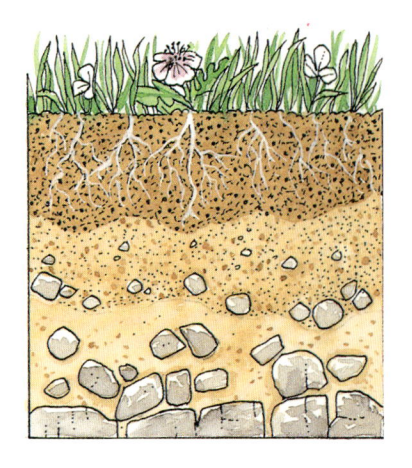

The things we usually think of as "riches of the Earth" are minerals. They are the basic raw materials for many of our industries, and digging them out of the Earth, processing them and shipping them around the world is a huge international business.

Minerals are all around us. Our cars are made mainly of steel, made from *iron*. They have *chrome* trim, *asbestos* in the brakes, *lead* and *zinc* in their batteries and *tungsten* in the lights. The windows of our houses are made from *silica* sand, and our electricity flows through *copper* cables. We write with pencils made of *graphite*, and sprinkle our food with *sodium chloride*.

The power that provides our heating and light also comes from underground mineral deposits. Coal is mined for use in houses and to fuel the furnaces of power stations. Oil and gas from beneath the land and sea provide more heating and generating power. And the oil itself is the raw material for a huge chemical industry making everything from cosmetics to gasoline, pesticides, plastics and drugs.

△ Huge excavating machines are used to dig coal from shallow deposits. The method is called strip mining. Once the coal is removed, the soil is put back and the farmland is restored.

▽ Blazing flares like these in the oilfields of Bahrain are used to burn off excess petroleum gas from the oil wells.

Glossary

Altitude Height above sea level.

Ammonite A tentacled sea animal that lived in a tightly coiled shell. Their shells are often preserved as fossils.

Ash Volcanic ash consists of small droplets of lava blown into the air by the force of an eruption.

Axis An imaginary line through the center of a planet, joining the north and south poles.

Basalt A very dark, fine-grained igneous rock. The mineral crystals are usually too small to be seen without a magnifying lens.

Batholith The largest kind of igneous intrusion. Batholiths often cover hundreds of square kilometers and are so deep that their lower limits are unknown.

Calcite Calcium carbonate. The main mineral in limestone rock. Also occurs in some igneous rocks and may form very large crystals. Most animal shells are made of this mineral.

Condense Change from a gas or vapor into a liquid. (Water in your breath will condense into a mist of fine droplets when you breathe on cold glass.)

Core The central zone of the Earth. It consists mainly of iron, with some silica and sulfur.

Crust The outer solid skin of the Earth. If you drew a 10-cm (4-in) diameter circle and let that represent the Earth, the entire thickness of the crust would fall within the thickness of the pencil line.

Depression An alternative name for a low-pressure weather system.

Eclipse Means "covering up." In a *solar eclipse* the Moon passes between Sun and Earth casting a shadow on the Earth. In a *lunar eclipse* the Earth passes between the Sun and Moon and casts a shadow on the Moon.

Ecosystem A complete living system of plants and animals all living in the same place.

Element The simplest form of chemical substance.

Equator The imaginary line encircling the Earth's surface midway between the north and south poles.

Extrusive The word means "forced out," and is used to describe rocks forced out on to the surface by volcanic eruptions.

Flash flood A sudden violent flood that follows rain in desert regions. The ground is baked so hard that water cannot sink in. Instead it rushes over the surface causing severe erosion.

Front A word used by meteorologists (weather scientists) to describe the boundary between areas of warm and cool air.

Galaxy A large group of stars. Each galaxy is separated from the next by a vast distance of empty space.

Glacier A slowly moving river of ice that flows down the side of a mountain under its own weight.

Granite A light-colored igneous rock. It is very hard and is often used as a building stone.

Gravity The invisible force of attraction that pulls a small light object toward a larger heavier object. The huge force of the Sun's gravitational pull holds all the planets in their orbits. Earth's gravity holds us in place on the surface.

Hemisphere Half a sphere. We use the terms northern hemisphere and southern hemisphere to describe the areas lying north and south of the Equator.

Humus The dark material in soil. It consists of the decayed remains of plants that have died, plus animal droppings. Humus is very important as it returns valuable chemicals back to the soil. It also binds the soil together and helps to hold water in the soil.

Igneous rocks All the rock types formed by volcanic activity, both on the surface and deep inside the crust.

Intrusive The word means "forced in" and is used to describe igneous rocks that have been forced in amongst other rocks.

Lava Molten rock poured out on to the surface of the Earth or the Moon usually in volcanic eruptions.

Light year The distance that light can travel in a year, roughly 9.5 million million km (5.9 million million miles). It is a convenient unit in which to measure the huge distances in space.

Lunar Anything to do with the Moon.

Mantle The thick layer of part-solid and part-molten rock lying beneath the Earth's crust. Churning movements in the mantle provide the force that moves the continents over the Earth's surface.

Metamorphic rocks Rocks that have been altered by heat or pressure. Marble, for example, is altered limestone.

Meteorite A fragment of rock traveling through space. Meteorites can be millions of tons in weight but most are like grains of sand. Small meteorites burn up when they enter the Earth's atmosphere. We sometimes see them as shooting stars.

Mineral A natural combination of elements that always has the same composition. There are about 2,000 different minerals.

Ore A kind of rock that is rich in a particular useful mineral and is mined so that the mineral can be extracted.

Saturated Means "holding as much as it can." When air is saturated with water vapor, any excess water will condense as droplets and form clouds, mist or fog.

Savanna A particular type of grassland vegetation found in Africa. It consists of large areas of long grass with scattered groups of trees.

Sedimentary rocks Rocks like sandstone, mudstone and chalk, formed when particles of eroded rock material or the remains of marine animals pile up on the seabed and later turn into rock.

Solar System The Sun's local system of nine orbiting planets and their moons.

Species A particular type of animal which can only breed with another of exactly the same type. For example, tigers and domestic cats are both members of the cat family but they are different species.

Tundra The special kind of vegetation found in the Arctic. Although the ground is frozen, a thin surface layer softens in summer allowing mosses and lichens to grow. Very similar vegetation is found on the tops of high mountains where the soil is thin and the temperatures very cold.

Weathering The first stage in erosion, in which the bare rock is softened and broken up by slightly acid rain water, big changes in temperature, and other processes.

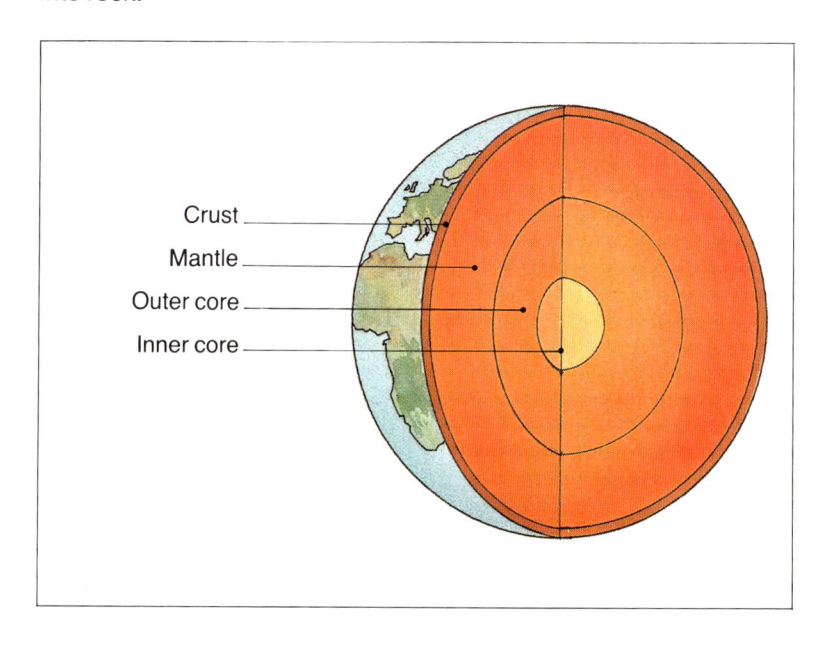

Crust
Mantle
Outer core
Inner core

31

Index

Aldrin, Edwin, 7
altitude 13, 30
amethyst 23
ammonite 20, 27, 30
animal life 18, 19
Armstrong, Neil, 7
asbestos 23, 29
ash 24, 30
asteroid 5
atmosphere 4, 6, 7, 12–13
axis 5, 9, 30

basalt 23, 24, 30
batholith 25, 30

calcite 27, 30
carbon 22
chalk 27
climate 18, 19
clouds 14, 15
coal 29
continents, movement of, 18, 21
core 6, 30
crust 6, 25, 30
crystals 22, 23

delta 17
depression 15, 30
desert 17, 18, 19, 28
diamond 22
dinosaurs 21
dyke 25

eclipse 7, 30
ecosystem 18, 30
element 22, 23, 30
Equator 9, 12, 30
erosion 16–17, 20, 25, 26
extrusive rocks 24, 30

feldspar 23
flash flood 16, 30
fossils 20–1, 27
front 15, 30

galaxy 4, 30
gas 29
geode 23
glacier 16, 30
gold 22, 23
granite 23, 25, 30
grassland 18
gravity 12, 30
gypsum 23

hematite 22
hemisphere 9, 30
high-pressure system 14–15
humus 28, 30

igneous rocks 24, 25, 26, 30
intrusive rocks 24, 25, 31
iron 22, 29

Jupiter 5, 7

lava 7, 24, 31
light year 4, 31
low-pressure system 14–15
lunar 7, 31

mantle 6, 31
Mars 4, 5, 7
Mercury 4, 5
mesosphere 13
metamorphic rocks 27, 31
meteorite 7, 31
mica 23
Milky Way 4
mineral 22–3, 29, 31
mining 29
Moon 5, 7

Neptune 5

ocean currents 10, 11
oceans 10–11
oil 29
ore 22, 31
oxygen 4, 12, 13, 22

planets 4–5, 6
plant life 18, 19
plateau 24
Pluto 5
pollution 13
pyrite 22

quartz 22, 23

radiation 13
rainforest 8, 19

salt 22
saturated air 14, 31
Saturn 5
savanna 18, 19, 31
seasons 8–9, 14, 15
sedimentary rocks 20, 21, 22, 26, 27, 31
silicon 22
sill 24, 25
slate 27
soil 28
Solar System 4–5, 6, 31
species 19, 31
star 4
steel 22, 29
strata 27
stratosphere 13
Sun 4, 5, 6, 7, 8, 9, 11, 13, 16

tor 25
tropical rainforest 19
troposphere 13
tundra 18, 31

Uranus 5

vegetation zones 18, 19
Venus 4, 5
volcano 22, 23, 24

weather 11, 12, 13, 14–15
weathering 25, 31
wind systems 12, 15